Where People Live

Kristy Stark, M.A.Ed.

Consultants

Mabel Huddleston
Tustin Unified School District

Publishing Credits

Rachelle Cracchiolo, M.S.Ed., *Publisher*
Conni Medina, M.A.Ed., *Managing Editor*
Emily R. Smith, M.A.Ed., *Series Developer*
June Kikuchi, *Content Director*
Susan Daddis, M.A.Ed., *Editor*
Courtney Roberson, *Senior Graphic Designer*

Image Credits: p.9 Courtesy of The New York Public Library; p.17 Courtesy of the Library of Congress LC-USF34-054438-E; p.24 (left) Jason Barles; p.24 (right) Allan Hack]; all other images from iStock and/or Shutterstock.

Library of Congress Cataloging-in-Publication Data

Names: Stark, Kristy, author.
Title: Where people live / Kristy Stark.
Description: Huntington Beach, CA : Teacher Created Materials, [2018] | Includes index. | Audience: K to Grade 3.
Identifiers: LCCN 2017053269 (print) | LCCN 2018007126 (ebook) | ISBN 9781425825584 | ISBN 9781425825164 (pbk.)
Subjects: LCSH: Human geography--Juvenile literature.
Classification: LCC GF48 (ebook) | LCC GF48 .S72 2018 (print) | DDC 304.2--dc23
LC record available at https://lccn.loc.gov/2017053269

Teacher Created Materials
5301 Oceanus Drive
Huntington Beach, CA 92649-1030
www.tcmpub.com
ISBN 978-1-4258-2516-4
© 2018 Teacher Created Materials, Inc.

Table of Contents

One Nation, Many Places to Live

The United States has many places to live. It has beaches and cliffs. It has fields and hills. It has small towns and big cities, too.

People live in all these places. But why do people live where they do? What makes a person choose to live near large fields instead of tall buildings?

New York City

City Life

Lots of people choose to live in big cities. New York City is big. More people live there than in any other U.S. city!

Living Off the Land

Some people choose where to live by the **features** of the land. American Indians were the first people in the United States. Some **tribes** built homes near the sea. They made large boats. They hunted whales in the sea. They ate the meat. They used parts of the whale for oil.

Love of Nature

American Indians showed people a different way to think. They had respect for the land. They fished and hunted only what they could eat and use. Some tribes thanked the plants and animals for their food.

American Indians used nets or spears to catch fish.

Then, people from other nations came. They first lived on the coast. But, they wanted more land. They moved closer to forests and rivers. Their homes were made from logs. They hunted bison, deer, and beaver. The furs were sold or traded.

Settlers used logs from the forest to build their homes.

Settlers hunted bison for their furs and meat.

City Life

More people moved to the United States. They hoped to make better lives. Some people stayed in the cities when they arrived. At first, it seemed scary in these new places. Then, they found homes close to people from their **native** nations. That put them near others who spoke the same languages. They shared the same **customs**. It made them feel safer.

Some people traveled on ships to the United States.

People from China moved into neighborhoods close to each other.

People found jobs. Some people sewed clothes. Others worked with steel in factories. There were jobs in shops that sold these things. Some cities became crowded.

So, people moved west. They built more cities. More jobs opened up. There were jobs in mining. People also worked on the railroads. The nation grew larger.

Women in cities sewed clothes in shops.

Fun and Games

Children used to play with homemade toys. Then, factories started making toys. People could buy toy trains. Crayons were invented. Bikes were made safer. More families could buy them.

The railroad moved goods and people much faster than before.

Country Life

Some people wanted more land. So, they moved to the **Plains** and started farms. Farmers grew wheat and corn. These crops grew well in this region. The summers were long and hot. The winters could be freezing.

MONTANA

NORTH DAKOTA

SOUTH DAKOTA

WYOMING

NEBRASKA

COLORADO

KANSAS

OKLAHOMA

NEW MEXICO

TEXAS

The Plains are located in
the middle of the country.

Some people moved south. The **climate** was warm there. The winters were mild. Farmers in the South planted a lot of cotton. Others planted tobacco. Some of the farmers became wealthy.

The yellow states on this map are the South.

What to Wear

In the South, summers are **humid**. This means that people wear light, loose clothes. These types of clothes help keep them cool. People who work outside wear long pants and sleeves. They want to cover as much of their bodies as they can. Doing this protects them from the sun.

A farmworker takes care of the cotton growing in this field.

Making a Home

The United States is big. It has lots of places to live. People move around based on their ways of life. American Indians were the first people to live here. They lived off the land. Then, **immigrants** came. They built cities. Some people chose to live in these cities. Others moved to the country. These are all factors in how the nation has grown.

Scrapbook It!

Think about the types of places where people live. What are the features of those places? What types of clothes do people wear there?

Choose two types of places to live. Make a scrapbook page for each one. Cut out or draw pictures of those places. Show the right types of land features, clothing, or weather that are found there.

Glossary

climate—the weather in a place over time

customs—ways people do things

features—distinct or special areas

humid—having a lot of moisture in the air

immigrants—people who come to a country to live there

native—born in a certain place

Plains—a region in the middle of the United States

tribes—groups of American Indians who have the same customs, beliefs, and language

Index

Your Turn!

    Look at the two pictures. Think about how your clothes, food, and home might be alike or different in both places. Draw a Venn diagram. Write words in the spaces that show your thinking.